# HOMES AND FAMILIES
## Growing Up In Bible Times

Text by Margaret Embry

The author asserts the moral right
to be identified as the author of this work

Published by
**Lion Publishing plc**
Sandy Lane West, Oxford, England
ISBN 0 7459 2178 7
**Albatross Books Pty Ltd**
PO Box 320, Sutherland, NSW 2232, Australia
ISBN 0 7324 0548 3

First edition 1995

10 9 8 7 6 5 4 3 2 1 0

**Contributors to this volume**
Margaret Embry is Tutor in New Testament Studies at Trinity College,
Bristol. She is also a contributor to *The Lion Encyclopedia of the Bible*.

Alan Millard, Rankin Professor of Hebrew and Ancient Semitic
Languages at Liverpool University, is the consultant for the illustrations
in this book, and all the books in the series.

**Acknowledgments**
All photographs are copyright © Lion Publishing, except the following:
Neil Beer: 6 (above right)
Sonia Halliday: 13 (right)
Nigel Hepper: 6 (below left)
Zev Radovan, Jerusalem: 7 (right)
Clifford Shirley: 14 (below right)
John Williams Studio: 6 (below right), 8, 15 (right), 16 (left), 17 (below left)
Zefa: 14 (middle right)

The following Lion Publishing photographs appear by courtesy of:
the Biblical Resources Pilgrim Centre, Tantur: 2 (below left)
the trustees of the British Museum: 18 (midddle left)
the Eretz Israel Museum, Tel Aviv: 14 (left, above right), 15 (left), 16
(above and below right), 17 (below right), 19 (middle right), 20 (left)
the Haifa Music Museum: 13 (left), 20 (right)

Illustrations, copyright © Lion Publishing, by:
Chris Molan: 1, 2, 3, 4, 5, 6, 7, 8, 9, 10, 11, 12, 13, 14, 15, 16, 17, 18, 19 (left
and right), 20
Jeffrey Burn: 2 (left), 4 (left), 5 (left and right), 6 (left), 7 (left), 8 (above
right), 11 (left), 12 (right), 18 (above right), 19 (below left)

Bible quotations are taken from the *Good News Bible*, copyright ©
American Bible Society, New York, 1966, 1971 and 4th edition 1976,
published by the Bible Societies/HarperCollins, with permission.

B·I·B·L·E  W·O·R·L·D

# HOMES AND FAMILIES

## GROWING UP IN BIBLE TIMES

## Margaret Embry

A LION BOOK

# Contents

page 20

page 6

page 9

page 14

page 19

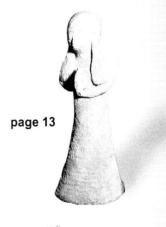

page 13

page 14

page 6

page 19

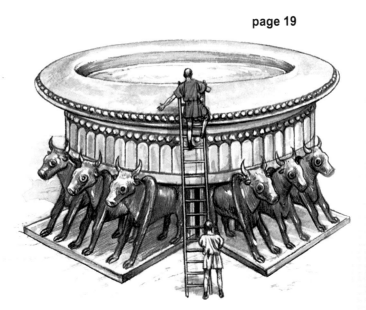

# 1 Families

Every child in the nation of Israel belonged to a large household. Parents and their children were part of a larger family group, including aunts and uncles and grandparents. Grandfather was the head of the household, and his word was law. Wealthy families had servants, who were also part of the household.

## The tribes of Israel

Near the beginning of the Bible story, when the people of Israel came out of Egypt to live in Canaan, they were divided into twelve large family groups called tribes. Each tribe was given a different area of the land to make their home.

Every child also belonged to a 'clan', the village or town where they lived. It was unusual to move away from the place where their family had made their home.

## Families

The Bible begins with a story about God making the world, and people to live in it. In the story God made a man and a woman. The plan was that they would be friends of God and that they would help and encourage each other.

But almost immediately, they disobeyed God. Their friendship with God was spoiled, and they began to quarrel and fight among themselves.

Not surprisingly, the rest of Bible history includes stories of families that were far from perfect. You can read about husbands and wives who were unkind to each other, and unfair in the way they treated their children. There are sad accounts of brothers and sisters being very cruel to each other.

But throughout, the Bible explains how God has always wanted to show people the good and right way to live: as friends with God and with each other once again.

### ▼ An extended family
This is how families often lived in New Testament times, with parents and children, aunts, uncles, cousins and grandparents sharing a group of houses.

# 2 On the Move

Nomads are people who travel around in family groups rather than living in one place. In Bible lands there have always been nomads as well as town dwellers.

## Abraham and the Israelites

Abraham, the man from whom the Israelites were descended, spent part of his life as a nomad. The first book of the Bible explains that he and his family grew up in a city called Ur. When he was a grown man, Abraham believed God was telling him to move to Canaan with all his household. They spent the rest of their lives travelling around the region of Canaan with their flocks, their servants and their tents.

This lifestyle continued for several generations, until the entire family group moved to live in Egypt, during the time of Joseph. They made homes for themselves in a particular region of Egypt.

About 400 years after that, the Israelites again lived as nomads for about forty years, from the time they escaped from Egypt to the time they settled in Canaan.

**◄ A well**
This well has a proper capstone. The hole allows a bucket to be let down to the water.

## Tents

The kind of tent nomads such as Abraham lived in looked like this. The inner tent was made of dark black or brown goats' and camels' hair. Strips of leather were sewn together to make a waterproof outer tent. Both layers were stretched across a wooden frame and held secure with cords pegged to the ground.

The front flap could be lifted to make a porch during the day. An inner screen separated the women's quarters from the rest of the tent.

## Looking for pasture

The nomads of the Bible lands depended on their flocks of sheep and goats to provide what they needed: meat and milk for food; hair, wool and leather for clothes and tents. They traded these products for the other things they needed, such as grain and wine.

It was very important to find grazing for the animals, and water to drink. If the nomads came near a town, they often needed permission to let the animals graze and to be allowed to use the well.

Sometimes they would find good grazing areas where they could stay a long time and grow crops.

## Welcoming visitors

A visitor was always given a great welcome in a nomad settlement. Father would bow as a sign of respect and offer water for washing. A child might be sent to fetch a lamb or a goat so that the women or the servants could prepare a feast, with meat as well as bread. Father would talk to the visitor as he ate, and would offer shelter for the night or even a few days.

Then the visitor would be accompanied for some way on his journey.

### ▲ Making do

In Bible times—and today—nomads had to make do with whatever materials they had for their tents.

### Water supply

In the hot lands of the Bible a water supply is very important. At each new campsite the men servants would dig a well. They would find a stone to place over the opening to stop sand and dirt getting in and to help stop the water evaporating away. At set times, the flocks would be brought to the well, and people would draw water for them in leather water buckets.

Groups of nomads often quarrelled about wells.

### ▼ The campsite

When the family found a good spot to stay for a while, the children or herdsmen would guard the animals while the women put up the tents.

# 3 Settled Communities

The Israelites began to make settled homes for themselves when they arrived in Canaan from Egypt.

There were already people living in Canaan, who had built cities for themselves. These cities were built with walls, to provide protection from enemies. There would be a few large buildings: perhaps a palace for the king or governer, and large homes for wealthy people. The rest of the houses were huddled together.

As the years went by, the Israelites built cities of their own.

## ▼ Meeting place

Just inside the gate was an open space. People would gather here to buy and sell goods. Some men would come looking for work, and those who needed work done would come to find the people to do it. Poor people would come to beg for the things they needed. Here, too, those who acted as judges in the community would listen to complaints people brought them and try to settle disputes.

## ▼ Fetching water

Women and children would go to fetch water. Sometimes this meant going down a flight of steps into the ground and along a tunnel to an underground pool that had been built to collect water from a nearby spring.

## ▼ Grainpit

People needed a good food supply. Cities often had special pits dug in the ground for storing grain—such as this one at Megiddo.

## Did you know?

Most communities had cisterns to collect water. A cistern pit was often pear-shaped pit and usually lined at the bottom with plaster so it would not leak. Rainwater trickled through the ground and collected in the pit. The narrow, funnel-shaped opening stopped water from evaporating but still allowed people to let a bucket down to collect the water. Some households had their own private cistern.

### ▶ Defences
Cities were built with strong walls. The gateway often had additional towers, to make it easier to defend.

### ▼ City homes
City houses were built close together. Some were used as shops or workshops.

### ▼ Greek and Roman influences
By New Testament times, both Greek and Roman styles of building and town planning were used in in Palestine. These often included a main street through the centre, shops and theatres, as well as a piped water supply. At Caesarea, a town built by Herod the Great, water was brought in by a long aqueduct.

# 4 Ordinary Homes

During Bible times, in lands where summers are long, hot and dry, many activities took place out of doors. Homes were typically just a few rooms built around a courtyard. The rooms were always rather dark—a place to keep things out of the rain and the sun, and a place to sleep and be safe at night.

**▲ Homes at Capernaum**
These are ruins of ordinary homes in Capernaum dating back to the time of Jesus. Jesus' disciple Peter probably lived close by.

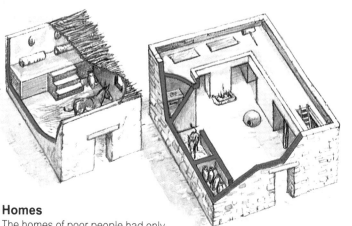

**Homes**
The homes of poor people had only one room, which they shared with the animals. There may have been a raised platform at one end, where the family would sleep. See how much bigger a typical courtyard house is.

**►Living quarters**
Rooms had little furniture: a table and chair and a lamp were ample for the living room. Many people would sleep on a thin mattress on the floor.

**A courtyard house**
A typical Israelite house consisted of rooms built around a courtyard. Some rooms were for stabling the animals, others for storing foodstuffs. Wine, oil and water were stored in large jars.

**►Food stores**
Grain would be kept in a pit lined with stones or basketry. A simple mill was kept nearby to grind the grain.

**►Cooking**
A hearth and an oven for cooking were often built in the courtyard, so the smoke could escape.

**▼ Water supply**
The capstone to a private cistern.

## Roof hopping!

The flat-roofed houses were often built so close together that it was possible to travel quite a distance across a town or city simply by stepping across the rooftops!

## ▲ Room on top

A ladder or staircase led to the flat roof. Here, figs, raisins or flax might be laid out to dry. It was a good place to call news to neighbours, or to lie down to sleep.

The roof consisted of beams overlaid with branches, and packed with mud plaster. A roller was kept handy to keep the surface well compacted. Even so, roofs often leaked!

# 5 Wealthy Homes

From the time that Israel had kings, some people began to get a lot richer than others. The homes of the wealthy were made from stone, not the ordinary sun-baked brick used for most homes.

They followed the same basic floor plan, but usually had more rooms. There could be two or more storeys: the ground floor was where people stored bulky items such as grain and where they cooked. There might also be rooms for animals. The upstairs was for eating and sleeping.

The wealthy made their homes comfortable with wall hangings and colourful rugs. They could afford carved wooden furniture, some wtih ivory inlays.

## A private room
It was a sign of great luxury to set aside a room for just one person! The Bible mentions that the prophet Elisha had a room of his own: a very wealthy woman who believed he was a holy man had it built specially as an extension on her family home.

## ▼ The Jerusalem mansion
In New Testament times the Romans ruled Palestine, and it seems that some wealthy Jews followed Roman fashions in their homes. A very large house from this time has been uncovered in Jerusalem. Underground was a basement, and two vaulted cisterns to provide water for the household, and large areas for storing pots of food and wine. There was a bath for ritual bathing according to the religious laws and another bathroom with a mosaic floor. The ground floor had several living rooms around a courtyard. Upstairs were bedrooms.

Elegent stucco wall and ceiling decoration—the latest fashion in New Testament Jerusalem!

The best painted pottery is brought out to impress important visitors.

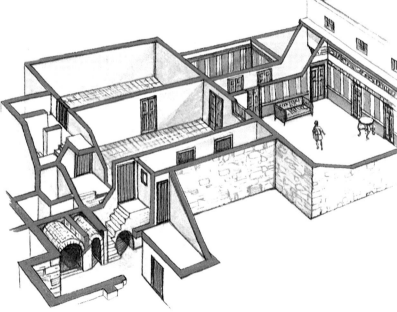

## ▼ The kitchen

The remains of the kitchen and its equipment from a wealthy home in Jerusalem around the time of Jesus.

## ▼ A party in the mansion

At one time, the main reception room in the grand mansion discovered in Jerusalem would have looked like this. Imagine how the owners must have felt when they heard Jesus warning people not to put their trust in their wealth!

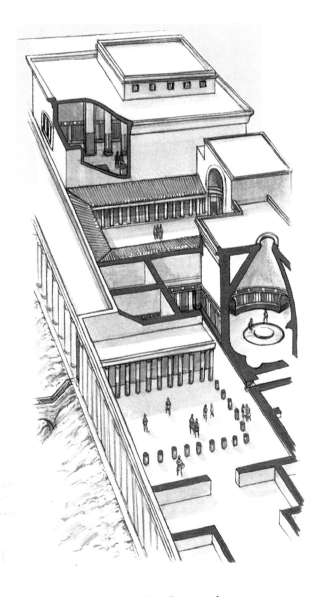

## ▲ Herod's winter palace

King Herod, who was the local ruler when Jesus was born, had a winter palace in Jericho, with elaborate baths in the Roman style and grand reception rooms.

The host shows off a fabulously expensive glass pitcher.

# 6 The Pattern of the Year

Throughout Bible times, many families had a small plot of land where they produced their own food. This made them very aware of the seasons of the year, and the work that needed to be done in each season.

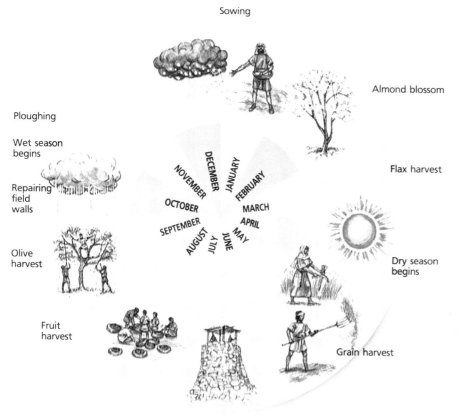

Sowing

Almond blossom

Flax harvest

Ploughing

Wet season begins

Repairing field walls

Olive harvest

Fruit harvest

Dry season begins

Grain harvest

Looking after the vines

DECEMBER JANUARY FEBRUARY MARCH APRIL MAY JUNE JULY AUGUST SEPTEMBER OCTOBER NOVEMBER

## Did you know?

Children had a rhyme, which described the pattern of the farming year:

The two months are (olive) harvest.
The two months are planting (grain).
The month is hoeing up of flax.
The month is harvest of barley.
The month is harvest and feasting.
The two months are vine tending.
The month is summer fruit.

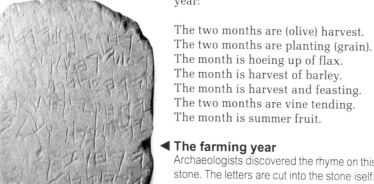

◄ **The farming year**
Archaeologists discovered the rhyme on this stone. The letters are cut into the stone iself.

▼ **Early autumn**
Olives were harvested in September and October. Terraced fields were mended.

▼ **Autumn rains**
When the early rains came in mid-October, people could begin ploughing. Once the soil was ready, wheat, barley and flax were sown, either in rows, or scattered haphazardly.

▼ **Winter chill**
December and January were cool and rainy. This was the time to plant vegetable seeds: chick-peas, lentils, onions, leeks, garlic and cucumbers, which would be ready for harvesting during the summer. By February, the almond trees would be in blossom: a clear sign of spring.

**◄ Spring rains**
Spring rains were vital for the fruit and vegetable crops to grow well. At this time, around March, the flax grown for linen would be ready to pull.

**► The grain harvest**
The dry season began around April. The wheat and barley were cut with sickles and bound into sheaves.

These were taken to the threshing floor—usually a high, windy spot outside the village. Here they were untied and spread out in a thick layer. Threshing might be done by driving a wooden sledge fitted with stone or metal teeth on the underside over the stalks. (See page 12.)

The mixture of stalks, empty ears and grain was winnowed with a fork on a breezy day to leave just the grain behind.

**► Vines**
In June, July and August people pruned the grapevines. As the fruit ripened, they would camp on a little tower in the corner of the vineyard, so as to keep a sharp look out for thieves, as well as to scare away birds or animals that came to raid the harvest.

**▲ Fruit**
During August and September, figs, sycamore figs, pomegranates and grapes were harvested as they ripened. Some grapes and figs were taken to be dried on the roof, for the dried product would keep a long time. Most of the grapes were taken to the town's winepress where they would be squeezed to make wine.

# 7 A Year of Festivals

God's laws told people to hold special festivals throughout the year. In all of these, the people were to remember how much God loved them and cared for them.

Booths

Day of Atonement

Trumpets

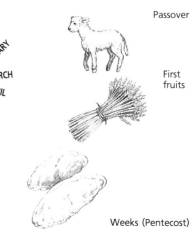

Passover

First fruits

Weeks (Pentecost)

## Passover
This was the most important festival of the year (see next page).

## First fruits
(March/April) The first sheaf of barley was offered to God. It was a reminder to the people that they should always offer God the first and the best of what they had.

## Weeks
(May) The end of the grain harvest was celebrated by a time of thanksgiving. The priest offered two new loaves of bread to God as part of a ceremony in the temple. This festival was later called Pentecost: it was the time when the followers of Jesus received the Holy Spirit.

## Trumpets
(September/October) Trumpets were blown at the beginning of every month, but in the autumn they introduced a month which had two important occasions: the Day of Atonement and the festival of Booths.

## The Day of Atonement
On this day everyone took part in a ceremony to ask God's forgiveness for all that they had done wrong. The high priest offered sacrifices and went into the 'holy of holies'—the innermost part of the tabernacle or temple—to present a part of the sacrifice to God. Then he took a goat, laid hands on its head, confessed the people's wrongdoing and sent the goat into the desert. It was a way of acting out the belief that God was taking away the people's sins so they could remain God's friends.

## Booths
(Tabernacles, Ingathering) This was the most popular and joyful festival, and came at the time of year when the fruit had been gathered. Families made huts outside—sometimes on their roofs—and lived in them. They remembered the time when their people had lived as nomads in the desert as they travelled from Egypt to Canaan, and they remembered how much God had cared for them. They also said prayers and held special ceremonies for the vital winter rain.

## ▼ The 'scapegoat'
The goat sent out into the desert on the Day of Atonement was called the 'scapegoat'.

## The Sabbath

*Work six days a week, but do no work on the seventh day, so that your slaves and the foreigners who work for you and even your animals can rest.*

The laws that God gave the Israelites reminded them to set aside one day in seven as a special day. It was to be a day of rest, and a day for worshipping God.

When the Jews were taken into exile, and were not able to go to the temple, they set up meeting places called synagogues. It became the rule that religious Jews would go to the synagogue on the sabbath to learn about God and to pray. At this time, they also wrote lots of extra rules about how to keep the original laws. Jesus criticized these extra rules: although they were well meant they were so hard to keep that they discouraged people from trying to live as God wanted.

## More Jewish Festivals

Jews today celebrate other festivals as well as the ones listed in God's laws.

Dedication/Lights remembers the time in 165 BCE when Judas Maccabeus rededicated the temple to God after it had been used for pagan ceremonies by a foreign ruler. The festival is called Hanukkah today.

Purim remembers the time when a Jewish woman, Esther, used her influence as the wife of a foreign king to save her people from being massacred.

### ▼ Hannukah

The festival of Hannukah lasts eight days. A light is lit for each day of the festival. The extra light is used to light the others!

# 8 Passover

The most important festival of the Jewish year was the Passover—sometimes called the Festival of Unleavened Bread. The laws God gave to Moses said how it should be celebrated.

> *In the month you left Egypt, celebrate the Festival of Unleavened Bread in the way I commanded you.*

These are the instructions for the first Passover—the actual night before the great escape from Egypt:

> *Every household must kill a lamb or kid and roast it. Eat the meat along with bitter herbs and bread made without yeast—unleavened bread. You are to eat it quickly, for you are to be dressed for travel, with your sandals on your feet and your stick in your hand.*

▲ **A Passover meal**
The traditional Passover meal includes roast lamb, a salad of bitter herbs and unleavened bread, which can be made quickly.

## A special meaning

It was important that everyone should understand the meaning of the festival. It became customary for the youngest child to ask this question:

*'Why is this night different from all other nights?'*

And the head of the family would answer, explaining that many years earlier, their nation had suffered as slaves in Egypt. The King of Egypt would not let them go, in spite of many warnings. Finally God had said that the oldest son of every family in Egypt would die. That night the Israelites were told to be ready to leave quickly. They had to kill a lamb and smear its blood on their doorposts, so that the 'Angel of Death' would see it, know that they were God's people and 'pass over' their houses.

And that is what happened. The king let them go. And God made a special agreement with the people, and brought them to a land that they could make their home.

## The Passover in Jesus' day

By the time of Jesus, families went to Jerusalem for the Passover if they could. They travelled there in groups and often sang special Psalms as they approached the city.

Each family brought lambs to the Temple courts, to be sacrificed by the priests. Then they took the animal away to be cooked for their own meal.

People spring cleaned their homes, as they searched through to clear out anything containing yeast.

They prepared the meal and ate together. The Roman style of the time, which some people copied, was to eat reclining at the table. There was singing and dancing as well as ritual words and prayers.

**▲ Priests and pilgrims**
Passover ceremonies in the temple built by Herod the Great—the temple of Jesus' day.

### Did you know?
The last meal Jesus shared with his friends before he died was almost certainly the Passover meal. He used the bread and wine which were part of the ceremony to explain to his disciples that he was going to die but that his death would mark the beginning of a new relationship between God and people.

# 9 A Marriage is Arranged

Throughout Bible times in Israel (and as in many countries today) parents arranged the marriages of their children. Usually the arrangements were made by the fathers. A boy was thought ready to be engaged (or 'betrothed') when he was thirteen, and a girl when she was twelve.

Typically, the boy's father would visit the family of the chosen girl and suggest the marriage. If the girl's father agreed, they would discuss a payment, or 'bride price'—for the girl's family would be losing a valuable worker. However, the girl's father would also promise a dowry. This would be a gift of money, land, or servants.

The fathers would sign an agreement, with other people there to witness it. Sometimes the boy and girl would send gifts to each other, but they often did not meet until the wedding day. This might be a year or more later.

## Single mothers

In Bible times, if a woman's husband died, she could be very poor. There were no pensions and she could not go out to work. God's law commanded people to take special care of widows and their children—and particularly so if they were relatives.

◀ **A coin head-dress**
Some of the coins from the dowry given to the bride's family might be sewn on to a head-dress similar to the one shown here. This showed them off—and kept them safe.

▶ **A wedding party**
The bride and groom sit under a special canopy, while guests dance to lively music.

## The wedding day

As the wedding day drew near, a first set of invitations would be sent out. A reminder would be sent to the guests once the preparations were complete.

On the day itself, the bridegroom and his friends went to the girl's house. She wore her wedding dress, a veil, and jewellery. She was surrounded by bridesmaids.

They would take the bride to her new home in the bridegroom's family home. Guests would join in along the way, sometimes forming a torchlight procession with singing and dancing.

On arrival, there was a party which might last for a week or more.

**A lasting relationship**
According to the Bible, God's plan was that a husband and wife should be partners for life. They were to help and encourage one another and to share in bringing up their children.

# 10 Family Roles

In the Bible story of the making of the world, men and women were created to enjoy friendship with God and to love and help one another. They each had a part to play in raising a family, and God's laws said that children should show respect to both their father and mother.

## Different roles

In Bible times, men and women had different roles. Women had an important role to play in the running of the household. This included producing items for sale at the market, particularly cloth. The men would be busy with a job that would also help provide for the family's needs—perhaps farming for food, or a trade that would bring in an income.

However, men and women did not have the same rights in Israel during Bible times. Women were regarded as part of their husband's 'possessions', and wives were expected to call their husband 'master' and 'lord'. A woman was not allowed to be a witness in court, and could not make a promise unless her husband (or father, if she was not married) allowed her to. A man could divorce his wife, but not a wife her husband.

By the time of Jesus, women were rather looked down on by the religious teachers. In the temple, they were allowed only as far as the first courtyard, the Court of Women. In the synagogue they sat with the children on a different side from the men or in a gallery. The rabbis would never discuss religious teaching with them.

## A good wife

This is how the book of Proverbs in the Bible describes a day in the life of a good wife!

*A good wife is more valuable than rubies.*
*Her husband has full confidence in her...*
*She makes cloth from wool and flax,*
*to make clothes for her family,*
*and more to sell...*
*With the money she makes*
*she buys a field*
*and plants a vineyard.*
*She provides food for her children*
*and the servants in her household*
*and is generous to the poor and needy.*

## Roles in God's family

Jesus astonished people by his attitudes to both men and women. He praised women and men alike for their faith. He welcomed those whom others looked down on—such as the man who collected more tax money than was necessary, and the woman who was caught having an affair.

The first Christians recognized that what Jesus taught about relationships was different from what they saw in ordinary family life. Anyone who believed in Jesus was part of God's family, and in God's family everyone had an important role to play. No one could say they were more important than anyone else.

### ▼ Partners

Women and men both did work that was vital to their families' well-being. Here, present-day women in Palestine fetch the water—as women did in Bible times.

# 11 A New Baby

When a new baby was born, there was a joyful family party. Children were seen as a sign of God's blessing. It was especially important to have a boy. Sons would keep the family business going, would provide one day for their elderly parents and continue the family name.

## A baby is born

A newborn baby was first washed and rubbed all over with salt, which was supposed to make the skin firm. The baby was then swaddled—wrapped tightly in long strips of cloth, with the arms straight down by the sides, to make a firm bundle. During the day, a swaddled baby could easily be carried on the mother's back in a cloth carrier—usually the woman's cloak, folded in a special way. At night, the carrier was hung like a hammock from a beam in the house or between forked sticks pushed into the ground.

The baby was 'changed' several times during the day. This involved loosening the cloths so the baby could be rubbed with olive oil and 'powdered' with crushed myrtle leaves.

Mothers usually breastfed their babies for two or three years.

▲ **A simple cradle**
A baby's cradle was rather like a hammock. It could be hung from a beam in the roof or slung between poles.

▼ **Celebrating**
Parents and relatives rejoice over a new baby.

## Naming the baby

In Old Testament times a baby was named right away. By New Testament times, the naming ceremony was not till the eighth day after birth.

The names people gave showed their feelings or hopes. Naomi means 'pleasant'; Mary means 'bitter'; Jesus means 'God saves'.

## Circumcision

God's laws said that baby boys should be circumcised: the loose skin on the penis had to be cut off. This was done by several nations at the time—and is something still done for a variety of reasons today—but for the Israelites it was a sign that the baby belonged to God's people.

## An important day

When Jesus was born, his parents took him to the temple in Jerusalem for two important Jewish ceremonies.

● **The buying back of the firstborn** The people were always to remember that, at the time the Israelites left Egypt, God took care of the firstborn sons, by saving them from death. The custom was that families would pay five pieces of silver to 'buy back' or 'redeem' their first son.

● **The 'purification'** According to the law of Moses, people must be 'clean' in order to join in the worship of a holy and perfect God. There were a number of things that made a person 'unclean', and having a baby was one of these. To be 'clean' again, the mother had to offer a sacrifice to God. Mary offered two pigeons, as the law required—the ceremony of 'purification'.

# 12 Growing Up

From a very young age, children in Bible times learned from their parents the kind of jobs they would do as adults. Girls learned from their mothers how to run a household. A lot of time was spent fetching water, preparing food and making clothes, as well as doing maintenance jobs around the house such as replastering walls. They also helped farm the family plot of land—particularly at harvest time.

Boys would learn the same trade as their father.

▼ **Girls and boys at work**
Here a young girl has been busy taking water from the well to her father, who is driving the threshing sledge over the barley crop. Younger brothers and sisters 'help' by riding on the sledge to weigh it down!

## ►Jobs for little children

Young children were often given the job of looking after the family's sheep and goats. They would take a stick and sling to help them drive off wild animals, and take the sheep or goats to a place where they could graze. At night, they would bring them back to the house or to the low-walled 'fold' where they were kept safe. Here two modern girls watch the family flocks to make sure no animals stray.

## Learning about God

The Hebrew scriptures include several reminders for grown-ups to teach their children about God: about the things that God had done for the people, and the laws that showed people the good and right way to live. Much of this teaching took place in the home.

In the centuries between the Old Testament and the New, the Jews set up schools. Most of these were in the local meeting-places, the synagogues, and were for boys only. The teachers were the rabbis. They taught the boys Hebrew, the language of the Old Testament, because by this time the people spoke Aramaic or Greek. The boys would learn to recite passages of scripture, there would be questions and answers, and the rabbis might tell stories to help explain the teaching.

 ### Did you know?

When Jesus was twelve, he went to Jerusalem with his family for the Passover festival. He spent time talking with the teachers in the temple. They were amazed at his understanding of the Jewish faith. He seemed to know more than other boys, even though they would all have gone to school to learn.

▲ **School in the synagogue**
Boys met in the school room of the local meeting place—the synagogue—to learn the scriptures, and how to read them.

# 13 Fun and Games

$M$aking a living in Bible times was hard work, but there was plenty of time for fun too. Every sabbath was a rest day, and the religious festivals were times for feasting and celebration. Family events such as a wedding or the birth of a baby also called for a party.

The Bible mentions a number of other special celebrations, such as the coronation of kings, and celebrations following victory in war.

**▲ Roman gameboard**
These playing boards for dice games have been scratched in the paving stones of the Roman fort of Antonia in Jerusalem. The soldiers who crucified Jesus may have played on these very stones.

**◀ Tambourine**
This statuette of a little girl shows that children have enjoyed making music from Bible times for centuries. The Bible often talks about playing the tambourine as part of making music to worship God.

## Children's games

Children played in the streets. They played games imitating grownups—having 'weddings' and 'funerals' and 'battles'. They practised shooting with home-made bows and arrows and with slingshots and stones.

They also had toys. Archaeologists have found game boards of ivory, with playing pieces of stone and clay. Other game boards were scratched on paving stones. Younger children probably enjoyed the carved pull-along toys that were made.

Children also played games with dice, balls, spinning tops, rattles and whistles. Simple musical instruments could easily be made at home, and children would have time to practise their skills when they were out watching the flocks. David, the shepherd boy who became a king, probably first learned to play a home-made harp while he watched over the flocks.

**▼ Playing at battles**

**▼ Board games**

## Stories and riddles

Riddles have been popular for centuries. Samson gave the Philistines a riddle to solve, and the Queen of Sheba brought some to try on Solomon, to see how wise he was. People also told stories both for entertainment and as a way of passing on the story of their people. Stories can be understood in many different ways. Jesus often told stories with hidden meanings to help people learn about God.

▶ **Taking good care**
A child carries his pet lamb to keep it safe.

▼ **A make-believe wedding canopy**

## Sports

Throughout Bible times it is clear that other nations enjoyed sports: the Egyptians, Mesopotamians, Greeks and Romans certainly did. However, many Jewish people felt they were wrong because athletes were naked and the games were performed to honour other gods.

## Pets

There is a story in the Old Testament about a man who had no cattle or sheep, but who bought one lamb which became a family pet. It seems likely that children adopted the young animals on the farm to love as pets.

▼ **Making music**

# 14 From Farm to Food

Throughout Bible times, most people produced their own food. They grew their own crops and raised their own animals for meat and milk. Some of the processes for turning the farm produce into usable foodstuffs were shared by the whole community.

### ▼ Winemaking
Grapes must be squeezed to extract the juice. One way of squeezing them was to tread on them in a winepress. The juice ran down channels into a collecting area. Then it was put in jars or new wineskins (which had 'stretch' in the leather) to ferment, and so produce wine.

### ▲ Grinding grain
Grain needs to be ground into flour that can be used to make bread and cakes. This grindstone mill from Bible times was turned by hitching people or animals to the wooden frame attached to it.

◀ **Pressing olives**
Olives had to be squeezed to obtain olive oil. This olive press uses donkey power to roll two heavy stones over the fruit to make the oily juice run out.

## Honey bees

The only sweetener available in Bible times was honey. Honey was collected from wild bees' nests in trees and rock crevices. But the Bible book called Proverbs had some wise advice to offer to anyone who found honey:

*If you find honey, eat just enough—too much of it, and you will be sick.*

## Fish

In Old Testament times only the people who lived close to a fishing area—the sea, or Lake Galilee, for example—could enjoy fish. By New Testament times, fish was salted to stop it going bad and sold all over the country.

# 15 Cooking

Cooking equipment in Bible times was fairly simple. Even the poorer family homes would usually have a fire to cook over. The hearth would probably be inside the house and the smoke would find its way out through the small window opening high up in the walls. In homes with a courtyard, the hearth was likely to be outside. There would be an oven there too, on which to bake bread.

**▲ Roast**
Meat might be roasted on a spit over an open fire. Such rich food was a rare luxury for most people.

**▲ A simple hearth**
In Old Testament times, a ring of stones would make a hearth for a cooking fire. Pots would be balanced on large stones placed inside this hearth, among the flames.

## Food laws

God's laws to the Israelites included rules about cooking and what to eat. For example:

● Meat had to be prepared so that the blood drained out of it. The blood represented life, which was sacred.

● A meal must never include meat and milk together. It was unthinkable that an animal should be cooked in its mother's milk.

● Certain animals and birds were never to be eaten. Pork, for example, was a forbidden food, as was shellfish. The ban was sensible in a hot climate, where the risk of food poisoning was high.

● Meat that had been sacrificed to another god was not to be eaten.

By New Testament times, religious people followed these rules very strictly. It was therefore difficult for Jews to eat with non-Jews. When both Jews and non-Jews became Christians, and wanted to share meals together, the leaders of the church had to think hard about these laws, and work out guidelines for the new situation.

**▼ A useful 'stove'**
By New Testament times, most homes had simple 'stoves' which had a fire underneath for cooking.

**▼ Popcorn!**
Ears of corn were sometimes put on a metal sheet over the fire to make the grain 'pop'.

**▲ The oven**
This type of oven was made from pottery or mud bricks, plastered with mud. A fire was lit in the bottom, which made the oven walls very hot. Bread was cooked on the hot surface rather as cakes are cooked on a griddle today.

## Bible-times bread

The basic ingredient for bread was wheat or barley. People would often grind their own grain— enough for their needs each day. They had to sieve the flour carefully to remove bits of dirt.

This would be mixed in a bowl with water or olive oil. For a sweet bread, a little honey was added.

Next they worked in a portion of uncooked dough kept specially from the previous day. This provided the yeast (people still use this technique, for 'sourdough' bread).

Finally, the dough was shaped into round, flat loaves and left in the warm sun to allow the yeast to make the loaves rise. One was kept uncooked, for the next day's baking, and the rest were cooked in the hot oven.

## Lentil stew

Lentil stew was everyday fare. The cook had simply to pod some lentils and put them in a cooking pot along with water, salt and any available herbs, such as mint, dill and cumin. This was boiled and then simmered until the stew was dark red.

Other vegetables, such as chopped garlic, leeks or onions, were sometimes added to vary the flavour of the stew. For special occasions, goatmeat, mutton or veal might be included.

## Yoghurt and cheese

Goat's milk was most commonly used in Bible times. If left in an open jar, bacteria in the air would sour it, to make yoghurt. If the sour milk was left longer, it would separate into curds and whey. The whey could be drained off, and the curds mixed with salt and pressed to make cheese.

# 16 Meals

For ordinary people in Bible times there was little variety of food. In a good year, there were plenty of herbs, vegetables and fruit to harvest and eat fresh from May to November. For the remainder of the year, people had to rely on what could be stored: grain for flour, dried grapes, figs and dates, or olives pickled in salt water.

Throughout the year, bread was the main food. Meat was eaten only rarely. Some families had a 'fatted calf'—a calf kept indoors and fed well, ready to be killed for meat for a special occasion.

**▲ Food for the working day**
Bread, olives, raisins and dried figs wrapped in a basket made a portable 'lunch'.

## A daily menu

There was no such thing as breakfast. Instead, people took food out with them—in a basket or cloth—to eat as they worked. A typical picnic would include bread, olives, dried raisins or a cake of dried figs pressed together, goat's milk cheese and water or wine to drink.

In the evening, families gathered round a large pot of vegetable stew. They took turns to dip their bread in it. There would be water or wine to drink.

Wealthier families ate meat more often. They could also afford imported foods, including rarer spices such as cinnamon.

### Did you know?

Providing meals for guests was an important responsibility. There were inns, but throughout Bible times most travellers looked for a home to stay in—whether the tent of a nomad, or a house. A guest was always served first and invited to stay the night. However, guests were not expected to stay more than three nights.

The Bible says that the baby Jesus had only a manger for a cradle, as the inn was full. The 'inn' may have been a kind of village guest room that everyone in Bethlehem helped look after, and where any of them could take visitors to stay. As Jesus was cradled in a manger, it seems Mary and Joseph had to make do with a room normally used to shelter animals.

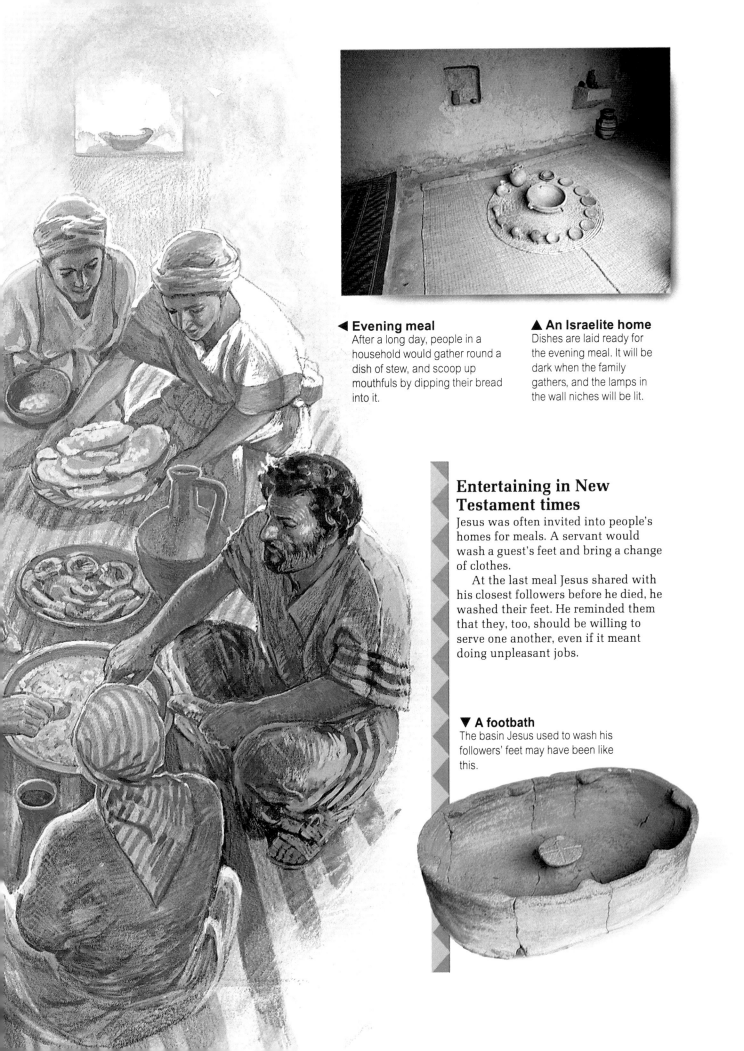

### ◀ Evening meal
After a long day, people in a household would gather round a dish of stew, and scoop up mouthfuls by dipping their bread into it.

### ▲ An Israelite home
Dishes are laid ready for the evening meal. It will be dark when the family gathers, and the lamps in the wall niches will be lit.

## Entertaining in New Testament times
Jesus was often invited into people's homes for meals. A servant would wash a guest's feet and bring a change of clothes.

At the last meal Jesus shared with his closest followers before he died, he washed their feet. He reminded them that they, too, should be willing to serve one another, even if it meant doing unpleasant jobs.

### ▼ A footbath
The basin Jesus used to wash his followers' feet may have been like this.

# 17 Making Clothes

Throughout Bible times most clothes were made in the local community. Some of the processes were shared—washing the fleece, for example, and dyeing it. However, the spinning and weaving was usually done by women in their homes. Women worked hard to produce extra cloth to take to market or to sell to merchants.

**?  Did you know?**

It is possible to weave a wide range of patterns and colours into cloth. Stripes and checks are easy to make, and skilful workers could produce much fancier patterns. Sometimes the cloth was embroidered. The richest embroidery included gold thread.

**▼ Wool**
The long hair of a sheep was sheared once a year to provide wool.

**▶Spinning combed wool**

## Materials

Sheep's wool was the material most commonly used for making clothes. Flax was grown to provide fibres for linen, which was soft and strong. The hair from camels and goats could be spun into thread and woven in a rough, heavy cloth suitable for rough outerwear and for tents.

**▼ Flax for linen**
The flowering stalks of the blue-flowered flax plant were pulled and left to dry, and the seeds removed. The dry stalks were then soaked in water to loosen the fibres. Putting the flax in running water produced fibres which could be made into beautifully soft cloth. Ordinary soaking produced coarser fibres, suitable for making into work clothes.

# Working with wool

The sheep were sheared once a year. This was a festive occasion!

First, the clipped wool had to be washed. Some families sent their wool to a person called a 'fuller' to have this done. The fuller worked well away from where people lived because of the smell. 'Fulling' means treading the wool in water to remove the natural oils in it.

Natural wool comes in different shades, with a range of browns as well as creamy-white. But often the clean wool was dyed. Purple was an expensive dye and highly prized, but red and blue were also popular colours. In some towns there was a family dyeing industry.

The wool was then combed, spun and woven.

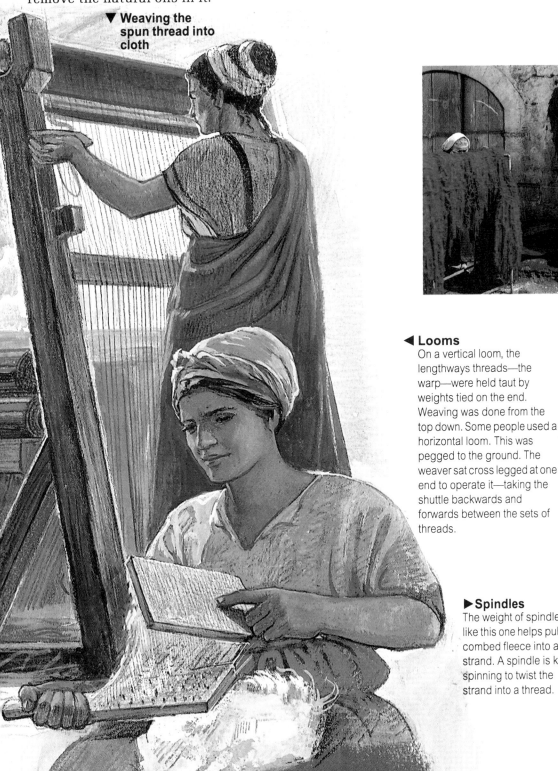

▼ Weaving the spun thread into cloth

▲ Dyeing
Here uncombed locks of wool have been dyed in the traditional way, and are being hung on a frame to dry.

◄ Looms
On a vertical loom, the lengthways threads—the warp—were held taut by weights tied on the end. Weaving was done from the top down. Some people used a horizontal loom. This was pegged to the ground. The weaver sat cross legged at one end to operate it—taking the shuttle backwards and forwards between the sets of threads.

► Spindles
The weight of spindles like this one helps pull the combed fleece into a thin strand. A spindle is kept spinning to twist the strand into a thread.

# What People Wore

eople have to choose clothes to match the kind of weather they get. The Bible lands have hot summers, although the nights can be chilly. The winters are mild, but sometimes it can be cold enough to snow! Throughout Bible times most people would have worn some kind of simple tunic, usually from shoulder to knee or shoulder to ankle. A tunic like this covered the body decently, and was easy to make with a rectangular piece of cloth from the loom. Children wore the same styles.

Making cloth from fleece or flax is hard work and only the very wealthy had more than one or two sets of clothing.

## Old Testament styles

There are few clues as to the styles of clothing worn by the Israelites. God's law said that they were not to make images of anything, so they did not draw pictures of people. There are only a few descriptions of clothing in the Bible itself. However, there are a few pictures that other nations made of them.

### New Testament dress

In New Testament times people's choice of clothes was influenced by Greek and Roman styles. The tunic was fuller than before, and pulled up over the sash at the waist. A folded woollen belt made a useful purse.

Everybody needed a cloak. Poor people could afford only a rough cloak of camels' or goats' hair, but most people had a woollen cloak. It could be worn in a variety of ways as a wrap, or sewn into a coat with sleeves.

▼ **Simple tunics**
This Assyrian engraving from around 2,500 years ago shows Judeans dressed in simple tunics.

▲ **Multi-coloured kilts**
An Egyptian painting from nearly 4,000 years ago shows people wearing these bright garments. They may have been the style for the people of Israel from Abraham up to the time of Joseph.

▶ **Sandals**
Many people went barefoot in Bible times. However, there were various styles of leather sandals.

## How to make a tunic

These pictures show three ways in which to make a tunic could be made from precious hand loomed cloth without wasting any.

## Tassels

In the Old Testament God's law said that all men were to wear tassels on the four corners of their cloaks, as a reminder of God. Later, these tassels were attached to a square woollen cloth worn under the cloak. Jesus criticized the religious teachers of the time for wearing extra long tassels just for show.

## Jewellery

Precious stones, shells, ivory, silver and gold were all used to make jewellery, including rings, earrings, nose rings, pendants, necklaces and bracelets. Wearing this kind of finery was part of celebrating a special occasion, such as a wedding. But writers in both the Old Testament and the New criticized those people who decked themselves out in order to get extra attention.

## Multi–purpose cloaks

A person's cloak was very valuable. For many, it was their blanket at night. It could be folded to make a bag to carry over the shoulder. Women folded their cloaks to make carriers for their babies. A cloak could also be used as a pillow, or as a cushion for an honoured guest to sit on.

# 19 Hygiene

People in Bible times rarely washed their whole bodies. Water was scarce and it was hard work drawing it and carrying it from the well or the cistern.

## In an ordinary home

It gets very dusty in a country where there is little rain, so the people needed to wash their hands, faces and, most especially, their feet.

Sometimes they used the ashes of burnt plants as a kind of soap. Soothing olive oil was rubbed into dry skin.

In Old Testament times men wore long hair and beards. They kept the law about not cutting the hair near their ears.

▶**Hairstyles**
In New Testament times many men copied the Roman style and had short hair and no beard. Women let their hair grow long, and wore it in braids or plaits. They sometimes wore their hair Roman-style piled on top of their heads in a hair net.

## Being clean for God

'Ritual washing' in order to make oneself clean for God was very important: a reminder that God is holy, and hates wrongdoing. Around Solomon's temple there were large basins of water for the priests to wash themselves, their clothes and their equipment before going into the Holy Place. In New Testament times, Herod's temple had special baths nearby, and some synagogues also had baths by the entrance.

Wealthy Jews had baths in their own homes for ritual washing.

# In a rich home

The rich spent more time and money on looking after the body. Perfume was used to cover up other smells. Rich women carried dry perfumes in little boxes, or in tiny cloth bags hung inside their clothes.

The rich also used make-up. They painted heavy lines of a black substance called kohl round the eyes. This helped protect the skin from the sun. They also used rouge on their cheeks, and lipstick.

Dye from the henna flower was made into nail varnish for fingers and toes.

▲ **Taking a bath**
A pottery model of a woman bathing.

▲ **Perfume bottles**

▼ **A wealthy bathroom**
A very large house from the time of Jesus has been discovered in Jerusalem. It had a bathroom like this.

# 20 A Death in the Family

It is always a sad time when someone in the family dies. People in Bible times were expected to show their feelings of grief openly. Children quickly grew used to people dying, because often brothers and sisters died while still young.

## A funeral

When a person died, the family wailed loudly to let other people know. Neighbours and relatives came immediately and the mourning continued for many days.

The body had to be prepared for the funeral on the same day that the person died because in a hot country, a dead body begins to smell very soon. The eyes were closed, and the body washed and smeared with sweet-smelling oil. In Old Testament times people dressed the body again in best clothes. In Jesus' time they wrapped the body in strips of linen along with spices and perfumes. A linen cloth was put over the face.

The men carried the body on a stretcher to the tomb. Coffins were not used. People followed wailing, often barefoot, and with ashes on their heads, and perhaps tearing their clothes as a sign of grief.

## The tomb

The family grave was usually either a cave or a tomb cut out of the rock. The body was placed inside and the tomb closed with a large stone, to keep animals out. Some rich people had very elaborate tombs.

In most places in Israel the soil is shallow. However, poor people were buried in shallow graves with a stone on top.

By New Testament times the stones which marked a grave or tomb were painted white immediately after the funeral. This helped people to avoid touching them, because a dead body was considered unclean.

Much later—after about a year had gone by—the tomb was opened and the bones were collected together, to leave space in the tomb for another body. In New Testament times the bones were sometimes put in a stone box called an ossuary.

**▲ Gathering the bones**
Once the flesh had rotted away from a corpse, the bones were collected into a small box called an ossuary.

## Life after death

In Old Testament times the people of Israel had rather vague ideas about what happened after death. Most people believed there was a rather gloomy place called 'Sheol' to which everyone would go. But by the time of Jesus some Jews believed that after death they would enjoy 'eternal life' with God.

The followers of Jesus had their beliefs transformed. Jesus was put to death, but a few days later, God brought him to life again—an event called the resurrection—and many people saw him. Jesus said that God would offer the same new life to anyone who believed in him. The followers of Jesus ever since have had this special hope.

## Mourning

By New Testament times there were people who were paid to be mourners: playing the flute and wailing. Jesus once came to the home of a little girl who had just died and the mourners were already making a real din. He sent them away . . . then he went to where the little girl was lying, and brought her to life again.

▶The sound of mourning
Pan-pipes were among the instruments played at funerals.

# Finding Out More

If you want to know more about what you've read in *Homes and Families*, you can look up the stories in the Bible.

The usual shorthand method has been used to refer to Bible passages. Each Bible book is split into chapters and verses. Take **Genesis 11:26-32**, for example. This refers to the book of Genesis; chapter 11; verses 26-32.

When a reference to a Gospel story has other references after it in brackets, this means that the same story has been told by more than one of the Gospel writers.

## 1 Families

| | |
|---|---|
| Genesis 1:1-31, 4:1-16, 11:27-32, 24:1-67, 27:1-45, 37:1-35; Micah 6:8 | **Families** |
| Numbers 1:1-54; Judges 6:11-16 | **The tribes of Israel** |

## 2 On the Move

| | |
|---|---|
| Genesis 37:25 | **On the move** |
| Genesis 12:1, 46:5-7 | **Abraham and the Israelites** |
| Genesis 2:16-20 | **A well** |
| Genesis 18:1-15 | **Tents** |
| Genesis 13:1-12, 27:5-29 | **Looking for pasture** |
| Genesis 18:1-8 | **Welcoming visitors** |
| Genesis 21:25-31; Exodus 2:16-20 | **Water supply** |

## 3 Settled Communities

| | |
|---|---|
| Joshua 6:1-21 | **Settled communities** |
| Ruth 4:1-12 | **Meeting place** |
| 2 Samuel 5:6-8 | **Fetching water** |
| 2 Chronicles 26:10 | **Cistern pits** |
| Jermiah 18:1-4 | **City homes** |

## 4 Ordinary Homes

| | |
|---|---|
| 2 Samuel 12:1-3 | **Poorer homes** |
| Matthew 8:14-15 | **Homes at Capernaum** |
| 2 Kings 4:10 | **Living quarters** |
| John 2:6-10 | **Food stores** |
| Joshua 2:2-6; Luke 5:18-20 | **Room on top** |

## 5 Wealthy Homes

| | |
|---|---|
| 1 Kings 7:1-8 | **Wealthy homes** |
| 2 Kings 4:8-10 | **A private room** |
| Luke 10:38-42 | **The kitchen** |
| Matthew 6:19-24 | **A party in the mansion** |

## 6 The Pattern of the Year

| | |
|---|---|
| Deuteronomy 24:20 | **Early autumn** |
| Luke 6:1, 8:4-8 | **Autumn rains** |
| Jeremiah 1:11 | **Winter chill** |
| Deuteronomy 24:19 | **The grain harvest** |
| Exodus 23:10-11 | **Rest for the land** |
| Isaiah 5:1-2 | **Vines** |
| Deuteronomy 24:21; Judges 6:11; Amos 7:14; Luke 13:6-9 | **Fruit** |

## 7 A Year of Festivals

| | |
|---|---|
| Leviticus 23:9-14 | **First fruits** |
| Leviticus 23:15-21 | **Weeks** |
| Leviticus 23:23-25 | **Trumpets** |
| Leviticus 23:33-36 | **Booths** |
| Leviticus 23:26-32 | **The Day of Atonement** |
| Exodus 20:8-10 | **The Sabbath** |
| Esther 9:1-28, 2 Maccabees 10:1-8 | **More Jewish festivals** |

## 8 Passover

| | |
|---|---|
| Exodus 12:3-11, 12:17 | **Passover** |
| Exodus 11:1-10, 12:1-27 | **A special meaning** |
| Psalm 15 | **The Passover in Jesus' day** |
| 1 Corinthians 11:23-25 | **Bread and wine** |

## 9 A Marriage is Arranged

| | |
|---|---|
| Luke 15:8-10 | **A coin head-dress** |
| Matthew 25:1-13; John 2:1-10 | **The wedding day** |
| Exodus 20:14 | **A lasting relationship** |
| Deuteronomy 24:17-22; Ruth 4:9-10 | **Single mothers** |

# Index